GOOD SPORTS
DON'T GIVE UP

By BREANN RUMSCH
Illustrated by MIKE PETRIK
Music by MARK MALLMAN

CANTATA
LEARNING

WWW.CANTATALEARNING.COM

D1515579

CANTATA LEARNING

Published by Cantata Learning
1710 Roe Crest Drive
North Mankato, MN 56003
www.cantatalearning.com

Library of Congress Cataloging-in-Publication Data
Names: Rumsch, BreAnn, 1981– author. | Petrik, Mike, illustrator. | Mallman,
Mark, composer.
Title: Good sports don't give up / by BreAnn Rumsch ; illustrated by Mike
Petrik ; music by Mark Mallman.
Description: North Mankato, MN : Cantata Learning, [2019] | "This text is set
to the tune of 'The Bear Went Over the Mountain'." | Includes
bibliographical references. | Audience: Ages: 5–7. | Audience: Grades:
K–3.
Identifiers: LCCN 2018053371 (print) | LCCN 2019008208 (ebook) | ISBN
9781684104154 (eBook) | ISBN 9781684104000 (hardcover) | ISBN
9781684104277 (pbk.)
Subjects: LCSH: Sportsmanship--Juvenile literature. | Teamwork
(Sports)--Juvenile literature. | Baseball players--Juvenile literature.
Classification: LCC GV706.3 (ebook) | LCC GV706.3 .R84 2019 (print) | DDC
175--dc23
LC record available at https://lccn.loc.gov/2018053371

Book design and art direction: Tim Palin Creative
Editorial direction: Kellie M. Hultgren
Music direction: Elizabeth Draper
Music arranged and produced by Mark Mallman

Printed in the United States of America.
0406

This text is set to the tune of "The Bear Went Over the Mountain."

ACCESS THE MUSIC!

SCAN CODE WITH MOBILE APP

CANTATALEARNING.COM

TIPS TO SUPPORT LITERACY AT HOME

WHY READING AND SINGING WITH YOUR CHILD IS SO IMPORTANT

Daily reading with your child leads to increased academic achievement. Music and songs, specifically rhyming songs, are a fun and easy way to build early literacy and language development. Music skills correlate significantly with both phonological awareness and reading development. Singing helps build vocabulary and speech development. And reading and appreciating music together is a wonderful way to strengthen your relationship.

READ AND SING EVERY DAY!

TIPS FOR USING CANTATA LEARNING BOOKS AND SONGS DURING YOUR DAILY STORY TIME

1. As you sing and read, point out the different words on the page that rhyme. Suggest other words that rhyme.

2. Memorize simple rhymes such as Itsy Bitsy Spider and sing them together. This encourages comprehension skills and early literacy skills.

3. Use the questions in the back of each book to guide your singing and storytelling.

4. Read the included sheet music with your child while you listen to the song. How do the music notes correlate to the words of the song?

5. Sing along on the go and at home. Access music by scanning the QR code on each Cantata book. You can also stream or download the music for free to your computer, smartphone, or mobile device.

Devoting time to daily reading shows that you are available for your child. Together, you are building language, literacy, and listening skills.

Have fun reading and singing!

What does it mean to not give up? It means that you try more than once. When you want to learn a new **skill**, you must **practice** it over and over until you **succeed**. Some things take time to learn. But the work is worth it!

When you don't give up, you are being a good sport. When you don't give up, you can do more than before. To see what happens when some baseball players don't give up, turn the page and sing along!

We want to learn, so we practice.
New skills can take lots of practice.

But don't give up! Let's all practice.
We try until we succeed!

When learning something new,
the team can get you through.

At practice, your **teammates** work with you.
You can help out your friends, too.

Together you'll work and get better.
That's what good sports would do.

We want to learn, so we practice.
New skills can take lots of practice.

But don't give up! Let's all practice.
We try until we succeed!

If at first you don't succeed,
more practice is what you need.

What skills would you like to do better?
Practice them over and over.

Don't give up. You can do it!
You'll get stronger than you were.

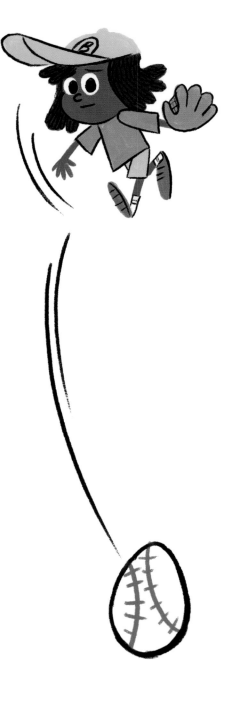

We want to learn, so we practice.
New skills can take lots of practice.

But don't give up! Let's all practice.
We try until we succeed!

At times we need more help.

It's okay to ask for help!

Helping you grow is what **coaches** do.

They teach you the rules and new moves, too.

As you learn all these cool skills,

your coach will cheer for you!

We want to learn, so we practice.
New skills can take lots of practice.

But don't give up! Let's all practice.
We try until we succeed!

At work and school and play,
we practice every day.

We have worked hard to **improve**.
Our team can use all its new moves.

We didn't give up. We got better!
We're proud of what we do.

Don't give up! When we practice,
it's amazing what we can do!

SONG LYRICS
Good Sports Don't Give Up

We want to learn, so we practice.
New skills can take lots of practice.
But don't give up! Let's all practice.
We try until we succeed!

When learning something new,
the team can get you through.
At practice, your teammates work with you.
You can help out your friends, too.
Together you'll work and get better.
That's what good sports would do.

We want to learn, so we practice.
New skills can take lots of practice.
But don't give up! Let's all practice.
We try until we succeed!

If at first you don't succeed,
more practice is what you need.
What skills would you like to do better?
Practice them over and over.
Don't give up. You can do it!
You'll get stronger than you were.

We want to learn, so we practice.
New skills can take lots of practice.
But don't give up! Let's all practice.
We try until we succeed!

At times we need more help.
It's okay to ask for help!
Helping you grow is what coaches do.
They teach you the rules and new moves, too.
As you learn all these cool skills,
your coach will cheer for you!

We want to learn, so we practice.
New skills can take lots of practice.
But don't give up! Let's all practice.
We try until we succeed!

At work and school and play,
we practice every day.
We have worked hard to improve.
Our team can use all its new moves.
We didn't give up. We got better!
We're proud of what we do.

Don't give up! When we practice,
it's amazing what we can do!

Good Sports Don't Give Up

Pop / Hip Hop
Mark Mallman

Chorus

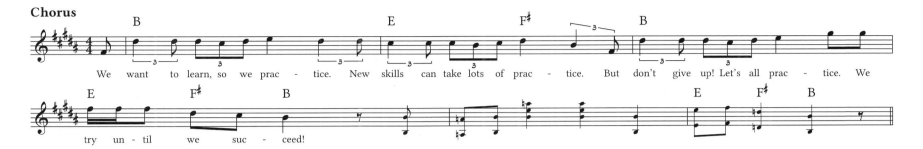

We want to learn, so we prac - tice. New skills can take lots of prac - tice. But don't give up! Let's all prac - tice. We

try un - til we suc - ceed!

Verse

1. When learn - ing some - thing new, the team can get you through. At prac - tice, your team - mates work with you.

You can help out your friends, too. To - geth - er you'll work and get bet - ter. That's what good sports would do.

Chorus

Verse 2
If at first you don't succeed,
more practice is what you need.
What skills would you like to do better?
Practice them over and over.
Don't give up. You can do it!
You'll get stronger than you were.

Chorus

Verse 3
At times we need more help.
It's okay to ask for help!
Helping you grow is what coaches do.
They teach you the rules and new moves, too.
As you learn all these cool skills,
your coach will cheer for you!

Chorus

Verse 4
At work and school and play,
we practice every day.
We have worked hard to improve.
Our team can use all its new moves.
We didn't give up. We got better!
We're proud of what we do.

Outro

Don't give up! When we prac - tice, it's a - maz - ing what we can do!

GLOSSARY

coaches—people who teach sports

improve—to get better

practice—to do something again and again to get better

skill—something you learn to do

succeed—to do what you are trying to do

teammates—people who are on the same team

together—with each other

CRITICAL THINKING QUESTIONS

1. Have you ever tried to do something that you couldn't do right away? What was it? How did it make you feel?

2. After reading the story, why do you think practicing and not giving up are important?

3. Think about something you want to learn how to do. Write it at the top of a piece of paper. Next, write down the things you need to do to learn this new skill. Then do the first thing today!

TO LEARN MORE

Arrow, Emily. *Trying Again*. North Mankato, MN: Cantata Learning, 2020.

Bechtel, Mark. *Baseball: Then to Wow!* New York: Liberty Street, 2016.

Herzog, Brad. *Powerful Stories of Perseverance*. Minneapolis: Free Spirit, 2014.

Joven, C. C. *Baseball Buzz*. North Mankato, MN: Stone Arch, 2017.

Morey, Allan. *Baseball*. Minneapolis: Jump!, 2015.

Omoth, Tyler. *First Source to Baseball: Rules, Equipment, and Key Playing Tips*. North Mankato, MN: Capstone, 2016.